DATE DUE

FAQ
TEEN LIFE™

FREQUENTLY ASKED QUESTIONS ABOUT

Wii and Video Game Injuries and Fitness

Jeanne Nagle

ROSEN
PUBLISHING®

New York

For Ben, who plays Wii games with me,
even though I'm not very good at them

Published in 2010 by The Rosen Publishing Group, Inc.
29 East 21st Street, New York, NY 10010

Library of Congress Cataloging-in-Publication Data

Nagle, Jeanne.
Frequently asked questions about Wii and video game injuries and fitness/ Jeanne Nagle.—1st ed.
    p. cm.—(FAQ: teen life)
Includes index.
ISBN-13: 978-1-4358-5329-4 (library binding)
1. Video games. 2. Nintendo Wii video games. 3. Physical fitness for youth. 4. Exercise. 5. Sports injuries—Prevention. I. Title.
GV1469.3.N34 2009
617.1'027—dc22

                                              2009001046

Manufactured in the United States of America

Contents

1 What Video Games and Devices Can Be Used for Fitness? 4

2 How Can Motion-Based Video Games Help People Stay Fit? 16

3 How Effective Is Video Fitness Versus Traditional Exercise? 26

4 What Injuries Are Caused by Playing Fitness Video Games? 34

5 How Big a Part Should Video Games Play in My Fitness Routine? 46

Glossary 56
For More Information 58
For Further Reading 61
Index 62

WHAT VIDEO GAMES AND DEVICES CAN BE USED FOR FITNESS?

Chances are that you've played your fair share of video games. Most people have. Ever since they came on the market in 1972, home video games have been a very successful, entertaining pastime for millions of people. Over the years, game designers and manufacturers have brought more complex themes and realistic visuals to their products. The level of interactivity, which lets players and computer programs respond to each other's actions, has also reached new heights. These improvements have made gaming wildly popular across the generations.

These days, video games are moving into new territory. Electronic games that promote physical fitness are in high demand. Thumbs and fingers are no longer the only parts of your body that get a workout during play.

Early home video games had simple, flat graphics. Worse, they only exercised a person's thumbs, not his or her whole body.

Fitness-based systems feature consoles and accessories that operate only when the player is in motion. These games and systems work various muscles throughout the body. They can even make players break a sweat. These games and gaming systems are also increasingly being used to help people disabled by age or illness strengthen their bodies and minds.

Leading the pack in this health-conscious gaming revolution is Nintendo, which makes the popular Wii system and Wii *Fit* games. Yet Wii is not the only—or even the first—fitness-related

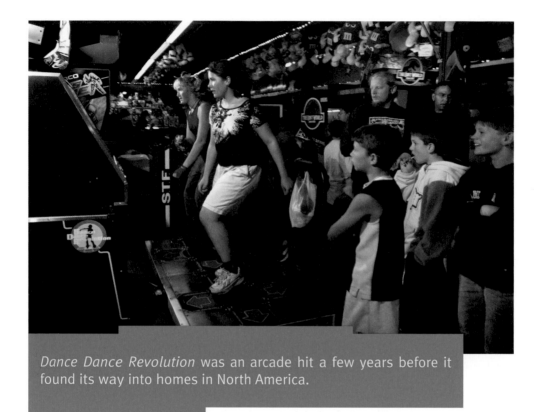

Dance Dance Revolution was an arcade hit a few years before it found its way into homes in North America.

video game innovation. For instance, *Dance Dance Revolution*, which rates players on their dance moves, had been launched as an arcade game in 1998. It was made available for North American home use in 2001, six years before Wii. Other early health-oriented video games were powered by physical activity. Joysticks and buttons were replaced with modified workout equipment connected to gaming consoles. Walking on a tread-mill or pedaling a stationary bike made the game run. Both *Dance Dance Revolution* and game-connected exercise machines are still available and popular to this day.

Do Fitness-Based Video Games Really Work?

How effective video games are at keeping people in shape, however, is a matter of some debate. After all, simulating a sport or activity isn't quite the same thing as participating in real life. Experts, including doctors, nutritionists, and physical therapists, do seem to agree that fitness-based games are more beneficial than passive games, where people just sit on the couch when they play. Plus, video games that require active participation might motivate players to get out and exercise in a more traditional way, without the help of a computer console and screen.

The main drawback to fitness-based video games seems to be that people might overdo the activity and hurt themselves. Common injuries, due to the same motion repeated over and over again, affect the arms, hands, and wrists. But other dangers lurk, too—anything from cuts and bruises to a wrenched back or sprained ankle.

Overall, though, video game fitness is relatively safe. In fact, when combined with traditional exercise and participation in sports, simulated workouts offer very real, not just virtual, benefits to your health.

Exergaming

When most people think of workout equipment, they probably automatically get pictures of barbells, treadmills, and cross trainers in their heads. They might want to add gaming consoles,

Fitness-based video games really bring out the fun-loving, active competitor in some people.

computer software, wired or wireless controllers, and television screens to that picture as well.

Highly interactive video games that require movement on the part of the player are part of what is known as exergaming. The idea behind exergaming is making exercise more fun, which motivates people to get active more often. Participants are challenged to complete a game-related task. For a lot of people, reaching an on-screen goal is a bit more motivating than simply staying healthy. So players may keep at it longer than they might if they just went to the gym to work out.

Exergames are available in a number of different formats, but they have a couple of concepts in common. First, some type of challenge is issued. Second, activity and movement are required to meet that challenge. Third, the level of play can be changed so that people with various fitness abilities, from beginner to expert, can play. Finally, exergame play is competitive, with players trying to beat simulated opponents on-screen, real-life rivals playing along with them, or simply their own best times and scores.

The following is not meant to be a complete list of exergames but merely a sample of some of the types of systems available, as well as the most popular.

Wii and Wii *Fit*

Launched in 2006, Nintendo's Wii has become a worldwide phenomenon. The system takes console gaming to a new level. The difference is in the controllers—the Wii remote and nunchuck. Traditionally, gamers have interacted with the action on-screen through the push of a button or twist of a joystick. Wii controllers,

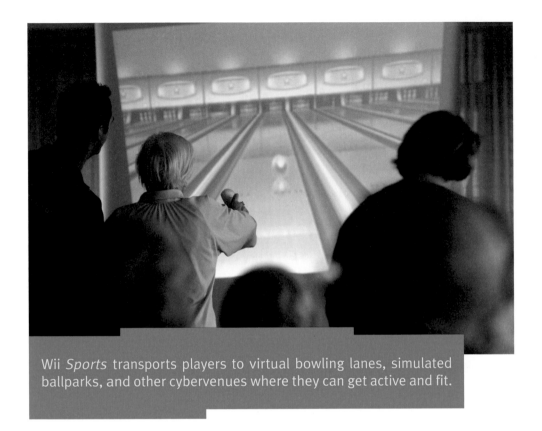

Wii *Sports* transports players to virtual bowling lanes, simulated ballparks, and other cybervenues where they can get active and fit.

on the other hand, use wireless sensors that read a player's movements and translate them to an avatar, or on-screen representation of the player. Instead of making avatars move through a control panel, players themselves move and the avatars (called "miis") mirror their activity on-screen.

A number of games are available for the Wii system. The most popular is Wii *Sports*, which comes packaged with the console. Wii *Sports* lets players simulate, or imitate, active participation in several sports, such as tennis, baseball, and boxing. Players move as if they are actually hitting a ball or punching an opponent while holding a remote or nunchuck.

Wii *Fit* was introduced to North American gamers in 2008. Dedicated specifically to fitness goals, Wii *Fit* has four categories of games: balance, strength, aerobics, and yoga. Bending, stretching, flexing, steadiness, and resistance within a target area of the body are the main goals within these games. In addition to the Wii remote, this system uses a balance board, which is another peripheral (meaning related but separate) piece of equipment. Players perform various activities while standing on the board. The board gauges the player's agility, or skillful ease of motion.

Dance Dance Revolution

Dancing is an aerobic activity that human beings have engaged in throughout the centuries, often just for fun. *Dance Dance Revolution*, a dance video game also known simply as *DDR*, adds a competitive edge that makes dancing even more appealing, especially to children and teenagers who enjoy playing electronic games.

Dance Dance Revolution was originally found only in video arcades, starting in 1999 in Europe and the United States. Players stand on a specially designed floorboard patterned with arrows. They try to match their footwork to a series of those same arrows as they scroll up on a screen in front of them. Electronic sensors in the floor record dancers' movements and determine how well they follow the pattern. All of this is done to a song that the player chooses.

In 2001, a home version of the game was developed for use with gaming systems like PlayStation and Xbox. There is also a Wii version of *DDR*. Plastic dance pads are part of the home-game package, but devoted players have been known to buy sturdier versions separately or even make their own dance floors.

Both the arcade and home versions of *DDR* have been incredibly popular. They get the heart pumping and have been shown to help players lose weight. This game may also minimize the eating of junk food, since players are physically active and less able to "zone out" (such as when watching television) and consume excessive calories. The home version of the game comes with a calorie calculator, so dancers can track how many calories they burn during each *DDR* session.

Virtual Biking and Hiking

Walking, running, hiking, and riding a bike are other forms of aerobic exercise that have recently received an electronic boost. There are exergames that use traditional exercise equipment plugged into gaming consoles. The exercise equipment takes the place of a controller. Walking, pedaling, and steering the equipment are the motions that make a variety of existing game systems run.

Stationary bikes are perhaps the most popular pieces of equipment that have been adapted for exergaming. GameBike, manufactured by a company called Cateye Fitness, is typical of these machines. The GameBike handlebars steer vehicles in racing and driving games, whether it's a car, bike, boat, or skateboard. On the recumbent, or reclining, versions, a wheel replaces the handlebars for steering. How fast the vehicle goes depends on how fast the player pedals.

Stationary bikes equipped with video screens provide interesting scenery and a convincing imitation of a workout in the great outdoors.

Even young players are getting in on this video-game bike action. Fisher-Price has introduced the Smart Cycle. The pint-sized bike connects directly to a television and plays learning game cartridges that come with the system. Both steering and an attached joystick are available as controllers.

Treadmills are also adapted for exergaming use. A machine called the GameRunner connects to a personal computer (PC) and runs a number of PC games. How fast a player walks on the treadmill determines how fast the on-screen action unfolds. The treadmill has a set of handlebars with buttons that act as a controller.

Giant Joystick, Big Muscles

Video game machines that use a type of exercise called isometrics are also available. Isometrics are exercises that build muscle by pushing or pulling against a stationary object. The range of movement is much less than that used during more typical aerobic exercise like running or biking, but there is still plenty of physical activity and exertion when performing isometrics.

Usually, isometrics are done against a wall or doorframe. In the case of exergaming, the stationary object a player pushes and pulls is a giant joystick controller. These systems, such as Exer-Station (formerly Kilowatt), are connected to a standard game console through wires at its platform base. Players control the game by moving the "steering stalk," which is typically at shoulder height. This stalk doesn't have the easy movement of a regular joystick. The idea is that players have to work hard to control the joystick and participate effectively in the game.

Because they are fairly expensive and tend to take up a lot of room, isometric gaming machines are not usually considered a home-use video game. Instead, they may be found in gyms or professional training facilities. For example, the U.S. Olympic Ski Team used this type of equipment to help get in shape for the 2006 Winter Olympics.

Getting into the Game

Isometric machines make players become a human controller, while Wii *Sports* and Wii *Fit* let them join the physical fun through simulation and avatars. Those who want to be a part

Players enter the screen and become video game characters courtesy of the *EyeToy* webcam. No avatar is required for games like these.

of the game in a more vivid, "real" way should consider exergames like *EyeToy*, which use digital cameras to put players on-screen in real time.

EyeToy is like a webcam, which captures images and downloads them through a computer or other network. The camera tracks players' movements and shows them on-screen in games designed for use with the system. A player's image is then able to interact with objects and characters in the game.

Most of the *EyeToy* games require a limited range of motion, since the camera captures only the face and upper body. One exception is the system's *Kinetic* game. "Kinetic" is another word for "moving." Like Wii *Fit*, *EyeToy Kinetic* features a series of exercise activities that players perform while trying to reach their fitness goals. To help players use their entire bodies, a camera with a wide-angle lens is used for this game. That way, lower-body exercises, which use the legs, can be shown on-screen as well as upper-body movement.

HOW CAN MOTION-BASED VIDEO GAMES HELP PEOPLE STAY FIT?

People who are not very active are often called "couch potatoes." Those who lie motionless like a lumpy spud in front of the television are the ones most likely to earn this nickname. The term has also been used to describe teenagers who sit on the couch and play video games for hours. Thanks to the popularity of motion-based video games, however, gaming and physical inactivity do not have to be linked anymore.

The key to this gaming turnaround is activity and movement. Video games with a fitness focus get people moving. Motion is absolutely essential to staying in shape. Without it, the muscles and bones of the human body get weak. The heart and other organs don't operate as well as they are supposed to. Overweight people tend to be less healthy in general and may be more

Lying around watching television may be relaxing, but it's not very healthy. Playing exergames is a better option.

predisposed to illnesses than are people of normal weight. Physical activity has also been proven to lighten a depressed person's mood and help children concentrate better in school.

Energetic motion is considered exercise, no matter when, how, or why it is performed. For instance, vacuuming, gardening, and shoveling snow tend to act on the human body in much the same way that going to the gym or participating in a sporting event does. Just about any movement done strenuously enough—with great energy and effort—for an extended period of time has benefits. That is why motion-based video games are perhaps a better alternative to mindless television-watching or passive video-gaming. Even the limited motion used during gaming is good motion. And it is certainly better than no motion—the inactivity typical of television watching or playing more traditional video games.

Physical activity falls into two main categories. Each affects the body in different ways. Aerobic exercise primarily works the cardiovascular system (the heart and blood vessels) and the lungs. Strength training, on the other hand, builds muscle mass. Playing motion-based video games involves, to a certain extent, both of these exercise groups.

Healthy Heart and Lungs

Aerobics were originally invented by an Air Force doctor in 1968 as a way to keep astronauts fit. Nowadays, millions of earthbound civilians embrace the concept, not just the folks at NASA.

Through periods of nonstop activity, aerobic exercise increases the body's ability to take in and use oxygen. The repeated motions performed while jogging, swimming, riding a bike, or similar exercise make the heart pump faster than when a person is merely sitting or standing still. Beating faster makes the heart stronger. It is much easier for a strong, healthy heart to pump oxygen-rich blood throughout the body. Small blood vessels, known as capillaries, help the process of transporting blood by getting larger during aerobics.

As the filter for oxygen absorbed by the body, the lungs also get a workout during aerobic exercise. Small sacs in the lungs, called alveoli, exchange carbon dioxide that the body doesn't

As virtual personal trainers remind gamers, the best exercise routine includes both strength training and aerobics, preferably in that order.

need for oxygen that it does. There are millions of these tiny sacs in each healthy lung. During extended periods of activity, the number of alveoli increases, which means that the maximum amount of air going into and out of a person's lungs also increases.

Video games that require constant motion for a reasonable length of time can provide an aerobic workout. A study conducted at Liverpool John Moores

Weights before cardio?
Or should you do your cardio exercises after a weight workout? The consensus is that weights should come first.

Makes lifting more effective
Gives more strength for weight workout, allows better loading of muscles

Reduces risk of injury
Do weight workout when fatigued by aerobic exercise, and you risk making mistakes and being injured

Burns more fat
1 Weightlifting deplete body's stores of glycogen (sugar used for "quick burst" energy)
2 Doing aerobic workout second burns less glycogen and more stored fat

Source: Mayo Clinic   Graphic: Helen Lee McComas, Paul Trap   © 2008 MC

University in England revealed that children's hearts can beat up to 130 times a minute while playing games on the Wii system—up from around 83 beats a minute while playing passive, or non-active, video games.

On the Wii *Sports* system, boxing is the prime aerobic game, with tennis a close second. Both of these games require that players use upper (arms and torso) and lower (legs and footwork) body movements. Wii *Fit* also features boxing, as well as jogging, hula hoops, and step dancing. Games powered by

Sparring in the boxing ring with Wii opponents helps players burn calories and sweat off the pounds.

activity, such as pedaling a stationary bike or running on a treadmill, offer the greatest aerobic benefit.

Weight Loss

Generating motion while playing video games has been tied to losing weight. Calories consumed when eating food are digested and stored in the body as fat until they are needed for energy. Because motion requires energy, physical activity burns calories. When an individual burns off more calories than he or she consumes, the result is weight loss.

The Liverpool John Moores University study found that playing Wii video games burns enough calories to help people lose weight. The university's researchers concluded that it takes more than twice the energy to play Wii games than regular, inactive console video games. More energy being used means more calories are being burned. Based on an average weekly playing time of around twelve hours—which is how long a separate study by GameVision determined average British teenagers play video games—Wii gamers are capable of burning more than 1,800 calories a week. At that rate, a person could lose up to 27 pounds (12 kilograms) in a year.

Other video games take a slightly different approach, making weight loss the goal of the game, rather than simply a positive byproduct of playing. My Weight Loss Coach, a customized program developed by the manufacturer Ubisoft for use with Nintendo's DS system, challenges players to eat right and get more exercise. The software rewards healthy habits with points, which are converted to miles. Players try to rack up enough miles to reach real-life distance goals like trying to walk as many miles as the Great Wall of China is long.

Strength Training

When done properly, aerobic exercise also affects the large muscles of the arms and legs. But to lengthen and tone the body's muscles, some form of strength training needs to take place. Resistance, which involves working muscles against an object that makes their movement harder, is what strength training is all about. Resistance is contracting, which means shortening,

Heading a soccer ball—even a virtual one—takes balance, flexibility, coordination, and overall fitness.

and then stretching muscles by pushing and pulling against some kind of weight. Handheld weights, large elastic bands, exercise machines, and even a person's own body weight all provide resistance.

Strength training is done in short, repeated bursts of activity called repetitions, or reps. The term for this kind of exercise is anaerobic. Because motion is involved, anaerobic exercise burns calories as well, just not as many as are burned during aerobic exercise. Mostly, though, the health benefit of strength training lies in building and toning muscle, as well as strengthening bones. Endurance, which refers to how long someone can perform an activity or type of exercise, also increases, thanks to strength training.

The majority of strength-training video games center on calisthenics, such as push-ups and lunges. Typically, resistance is provided by a player's own body weight. Wii *Fit* devotes an entire section of games to muscle strength. Players perform reps of exercises like leg extensions and torso twists at a brisk pace and with proper form, as determined by a balance board that records and evaluates movement. Performance is rewarded by points, which players try to accumulate in order to reach their personal fitness goals.

Balance and Flexibility

Most people know how aerobic and strength exercises keep a body healthy. Yet there is more to being physically fit than breaking a sweat or pumping iron. Movement and activity are next to impossible without balance and flexibility.

The U.S. Presidential Council on Physical Fitness has determined that balance is a skill that doesn't keep a person healthy. Instead, it helps individuals perform the exercises and maneuvers that do contribute to good health. Balance is necessary for coordination, which is when muscle groups work together to create smooth movement.

Flexibility, on the other hand, is considered health-related by the council. Being able to move the body's joints smoothly is what makes a person flexible. An abnormal range of motion can indicate damage or disease to the bones of a joint or the muscle, ligaments, and tissue that surround it. Like balance, flexibility is also required for a person to gain the full benefits of movement and exercise.

Wii *Fit* has a number of games specifically designed to help players improve their balance. In fact, since a balance board is used to monitor player movement during all play, it could be said that the entire Wii *Fit* system revolves around balance. All motion-based video games offer some kind of flexibility training because players continually bend and stretch their joints while operating the game.

Mental Fitness

In addition to physical fitness, video games exercise the mind as well. Shortly after video games were introduced for home use, researchers determined that playing them increases a person's hand-eye coordination. Recent studies, though, have proven there's more to it than that. Gaming can actually improve cognition, which is how a person thinks, analyzes information, solves problems, and gains knowledge.

Researchers like Professor James Gee of the University of Wisconsin have discovered that the way people solve problems and make decisions is very similar to how they approach playing video games. In other words, humans tend to simulate a situation—create a mental movie scene—in their minds before they take action. Also, gamers, like real-life learners and achievers, must master certain skills before they can move on to the next level. Gathering information in stages and meeting new, manageable challenges like this is how people learn best,

Games like Nintendo's *Brain Age* let gamers flex their mental muscles. Playing these "head games" is a nice complement to body-related fitness gaming.

according to Gee. Therefore, playing video games is like practice for learning and succeeding in real-world situations.

Cognitive, or mental, benefits can be gained while playing just about any video game. Yet manufacturers have made a point of developing games specifically for mental fitness. The maker of the Wii system, Nintendo, produces the popular *Brain Age*, which asks players to solve math problems, unscramble letters to form words, and draw pictures from memory. A similar package of interactive games and puzzles known as *MindFit* is made by a company called CogniFit and sold as "brain training software."

Chapter three

HOW EFFECTIVE IS VIDEO FITNESS VERSUS TRADITIONAL EXERCISE?

When an item or event is simulated, it is like the real thing but not quite the same. So simulated exercise through motion-based video games is an approximation of (similar to) traditional exercise and participation in real sporting events. Yet it is not quite as effective from a fitness standpoint.

The introduction of Wii *Sports* and Wii *Fit* created a renewed interest in the effects of video games on people's health, especially children and teenagers. For years, video games were thought to be the enemy of fitness. After all, kids simply sat in front of a screen and clicked buttons. There was nothing aerobic or strengthening about it. People blamed gaming, along with television, for America's children being so overweight and out of shape. Now that the new wave of interactive games has gotten people moving, however, experts are rethinking their opinions.

Still, the study of how beneficial motion-based video games are to a person's fitness is fairly new. There are only a handful of legitimate studies into how exergaming compares to true exercise. Evidence drawn from this research, as well as from the experiences of everyday people that are reported in the media and on the Web, suggests that while they are no replacement for actual exercise, motion-based video games might be useful fitness tools after all.

Active vs. Passive Video Games

One thing doctors, physical fitness professionals, and even gamers agree on is that playing active video games is much better for a person's health than standard passive gaming. The simple act of standing, rather than sitting, seems to give interactive games an edge. Judith Sherman-Wolin, a fitness expert at the University of California at Los Angeles's Center for Human Nutrition, estimates that sitting and watching television burns around sixteen calories an hour. According to Sherman-Wolin, standing raises the number of calories consumed to twenty. That's not much of a difference, but it does show that just about any kind of motion is better than total inactivity.

Several studies have shown that actively playing video games boosts fitness. Those who conduct the studies look for an increase in heart rate and the total number of calories burned to determine how effective active video games are at keeping people more fit. In 2008, researchers at the University of Nebraska compared Wii *Sports* with passive, traditional games. They found that two to three times as many calories are burned playing tennis and boxing on the Wii system versus traditional games that are operated by simply clicking a button. The heart rates of study participants, who were all around eleven years old, reached an average of 120 beats per minute. The heart rate of a person playing a passive video game is usually around 80.

Another study, conducted around the same time by researchers at the University of Glasgow in Scotland, showed that playing traditional video games used up about as many calories as sitting and reading a book. Dance-fitness and boxing video games, on the other hand, got participants' hearts pumping as fast as they would if the gamers were jogging.

Comparison to Traditional Exercise

While they obviously are better, from a fitness perspective, than watching television or playing passive video games, exergames come up short when compared to actual physical exercise and sports. Doctors and researchers base this conclusion on the fact that although there is a rise in heart rate and calories consumed during exergaming, it is not enough to meet the minimal fitness requirements that traditional exercise provides. In other words, more energy is used and more calories are burned when playing regular sports or exercising in a traditional way than when playing a fitness video game.

Several studies have tried to determine how effective motion-based video games are as a fitness tool. Some, like a

Tackling rugged terrain on a mountain bike beats both stationary bikes and video-based virtual cycling when it comes to getting fit and enjoying an adrenaline rush.

2008 study conducted by the American Council on Exercise (ACE), did so by counting calories. Activity burns calories. Therefore, the more calories that are burned, the greater the activity and fitness benefit. According to the ACE study, Wii *Sports* video games do improve aerobic fitness and burn calories. However, none of the system's sports used up as much energy as their real-life counterparts. For instance, Wii *Sports* bowling burns about 117 calories during a thirty-minute session. ACE researchers have determined that actual bowling, with lanes and weighted bowling balls, easily consumes twice that amount in the same time frame.

The study's results for Wii *Tennis* and *Baseball* were similar, while Wii *Golf* turned out to have roughly the same low-calorie burn (3.1 per minute) as an actual round on an outdoor golf course (3.9 per minute). Only Wii *Boxing*, which burned seven calories a minute, compared favorably with its real-life version of the sport (10 calories a minute) and offered enough strenuous exercise to improve fitness.

An exercise physiology class at Dalhousie University, located in Halifax, Nova Scotia, came to pretty much the same conclusion. As a class project, students decided to put exergaming to the test. They participated in three forms of exercise: Wii boxing, a more traditional "boxercise" workout, and walking. The student-researchers discovered that thirty minutes of Wii *Boxing* gives people a slightly better cardio workout than a half-hour walk. Yet compared to the boxercise workout, which is boxing punches and footwork set to music, Wii *Boxing* was less effective.

The Case of the Shrinking Blogger

Research indicates that motion-based video games by themselves don't consume enough calories to be considered proper exercise. Informal studies, conducted in living rooms across America, seem to claim otherwise. Devoted exergamers say that they have seen health and fitness results from playing Wii and other active games.

Perhaps the most well known of these experiments took place in Philadelphia, Pennsylvania, in 2006. Mickey DeLorenzo played Wii *Sports* for thirty minutes a day, for six weeks. He didn't change his diet or anything else about his lifestyle. He also didn't add any exercise other than the Wii. DeLorenzo posted his daily weight, which he checked three times a day, on his Web site. Many people followed his progress. At the end of six weeks, he had lost 9 pounds (4 kg).

Wii *Bowling* can help you lose weight and burn calories, but not nearly as much as the real thing.

More important, he had trimmed his body mass index, which determines whether or not a person is overweight.

Doctors and nutritionists—professionals who study the effects of what people eat—point out that DeLorenzo's experience is not typical. In an article on WebMD, Joseph Donnelly, a sport and exercise professor at the University of Kansas, reported that individual studies and experiments may show health benefits from exergaming. However, when applied to the larger population, the results are "not so good." So despite what exergamers may say, most experts agree that video fitness works best when it is added to a traditional exercise and fitness routine, not used in place of one.

Exergaming and Physical Therapy

There is one area where exergaming compares favorably to traditional methods of exercise: rehabilitation. The motions required to play many of the Wii *Sports* and Wii *Fit* games are very similar to those physical therapists use to help people recover from strokes, joint replacement operations, and spinal cord injuries. In fact, Wii games are such a popular rehab tool that some people have started calling the use of active video games in physical therapy "Wii-hab."

Building strength, increasing flexibility, and improving coordination are the goals of physical therapy. Exercises designed to achieve those goals are often difficult for therapy patients, whose bodies are weakened by age, a medical condition, or an injury. The low-intensity workout of active video games is a real plus. Patients go through the motions, but there isn't as much stress on their bodies as there would be during conventional exercises and activities.

Making rehab fun has other benefits as well. Playing games is much more entertaining than doing plain old leg raises or arm curls. More than that, interactive video games have been shown to distract patients, especially young children, from the pain and stress frequently associated with rehabilitation. With Wii *Sports* and Wii *Fit*, patients are more likely to remain interested in their therapy, stick with it, and see it through to successful completion.

A group of seniors participates in the Wii *Sports* Bowling Championships in Germany, an event created by college students impressed by their grandparents' enthusiasm for the exergames.

Hospitals, nursing homes, and rehab facilities are quickly adopting motion-based video games in their therapy sessions. In August 2008, physical therapists from fifteen countries met in Vancouver, Canada, to discuss using virtual reality as a form of rehabilitation. One of the main events was a tutorial on additional ways Wii games can help put patients back on the road to fitness.

WHAT INJURIES ARE CAUSED BY PLAYING FITNESS VIDEO GAMES?

The only sure way to avoid injury during any kind of activity is never to go anywhere, never do anything, and never even move. Any person who engages in physical activity, even of the most ordinary, low-intensity kind like walking, runs the risk of getting hurt. This is true even with the exercise people get when they play motion-based video games. Obviously, total inactivity is not advisable. The health benefits of safe movement and careful exercise outweigh the risks of injury that may occur.

Motion-based video game injuries happen for a number of reasons. What many fitness-based video game injuries have in common is that they are caused by motions that are repeated over and over again. These repetitive movements put a strain on muscles and tendons, which are thick ropes of tissue that connect muscle

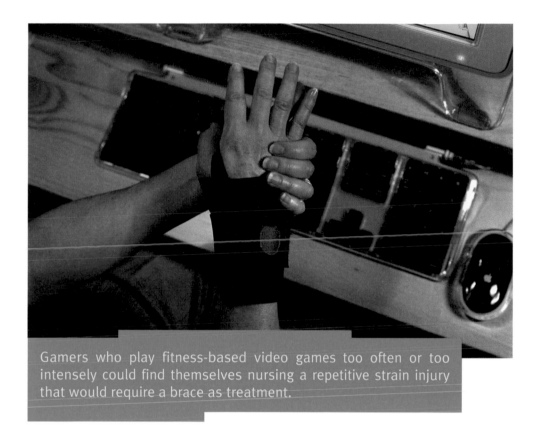

Gamers who play fitness-based video games too often or too intensely could find themselves nursing a repetitive strain injury that would require a brace as treatment.

to bone. Eventually, the wear and tear does enough damage to create a repetitive strain injury, or RSI.

The difference between simulating moves and actually performing them raises the risk of getting hurt as well. Sports like tennis and baseball are meant to be played outdoors, where movements have to be pretty forceful to cover a fairly large playing area and to effectively manipulate heavy or unwieldy equipment like bats, balls, and rackets. Not as much effort is needed to simulate the same movement in a video game system like Wii *Sports.* However, players don't always remember that and sometimes swing away as if they are hitting a ball or pitching in real life. Using unnecessarily intense body motions, especially repeatedly for long periods of time, can result in injury.

There is also a greater chance of knocking into furniture, slipping, tripping, or some other kind of accident occurring when playing motion-based video games. This is especially true when playing in a relatively confined and cramped area like a furnished living room or concrete and cinder block basement. Players may simply get carried away with the game. In their excitement, they might jump or run around and not watch where they are going, causing injury to themselves or others.

Typical Injury "Hot Spots"

Gaming injuries used to be limited to the few parts of a player's body that were active. Hands, wrists, and, of course, thumbs controlled the action while people sat in front of a TV screen to play. Exergaming has spread the activity around to different limbs and muscles by getting players off the couch and moving. As positive a development as this is, however, the number of possible injuries has increased as a result.

Which body parts suffer while exergaming depends on the type of activity being performed. Hands, wrists, and fingers are used to play motion-based video games as well as traditional ones. Therefore, these areas are still likely to get sore or injured while playing active games. But shoulders, elbows, the back, knees, ankles, and feet are now at risk, too.

Players who simulate sports may receive injuries in the same places as athletes who play those sports in real life. For instance,

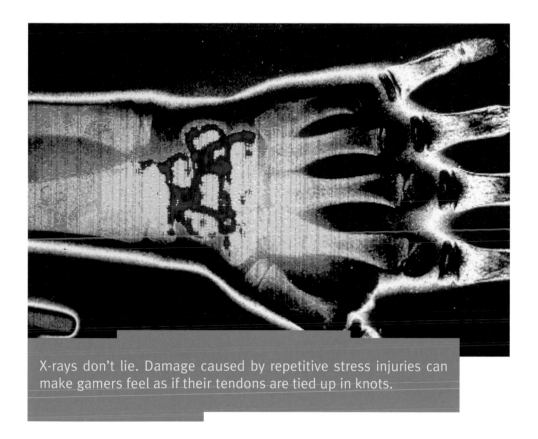

X-rays don't lie. Damage caused by repetitive stress injuries can make gamers feel as if their tendons are tied up in knots.

it is possible to get tennis elbow when playing video racquet sports because of the bending and twisting motion required.

Tendonitis and Bursitis

Doctors are reporting that many more patients are coming to see them with video game injuries, especially since the introduction of the Wii gaming system. Chief among the patients' complaints is tendonitis. This is when tendons become inflamed, meaning swollen, due to overuse or misuse. Sometimes, if the stress continues, tendons can actually tear.

Whether inflamed or torn, damaged tendons cause a great deal of pain and stiffness.

A similar video game–related injury that's on the rise is bursitis. Bursas are sacs of fluid located around the body's joints. They cushion joints so that bone doesn't rub against bone. Repetitive motion can cause the bursas to swell, getting so large that they can stop joints from being able to move. Pain, tenderness, swelling, a little redness, and skin warmth are all possible symptoms of bursitis. So many people have reported getting tendonitis and bursitis from playing Wii *Sports* games that doctors and the media (newspapers, magazine, TV, radio) have started calling this type of injury "Wii-itis."

Other Fitness-Based Video Game Injuries

Located in the wrist, the carpal tunnel is a small passageway housing a bundle of nerves, tendons, arteries, and vessels important to the proper functioning of the forearm and hands. Each arm has a carpal tunnel. Carpal tunnel syndrome is when repetitive motion in the arms, wrists, hands, and fingers puts pressure on the nerves and tendons, causing them to swell. Pain, numbness, and being unable to grasp objects are the result.

Carpal tunnel syndrome is usually associated with excess keyboarding. The wrists and hands are kept pretty much in one position, and they have to absorb the impact of repeated key strikes. People who play a lot of video games may also develop this injury through constant flicking of the wrist and the pushing of controller buttons.

Holding a video game controller at odd angles and making sudden, jerky motions may make you feel more involved in the game, but they can do serious damage to your joints.

Shoulders also frequently take a beating during motion-based video game play. Rotator cuff injuries, where one or more shoulder muscles become inflamed, are common. Motions in which the arm is lifted shoulder-height or higher can damage the rotator cuff. So can certain resistance moves, in which the arm is raised and the shoulder is in motion. Wii *Tennis*, *Baseball*, *Boxing*, and some yoga positions and strength exercises can all cause rotator cuff injuries.

As you may have noticed, most video game injuries occur in the upper part of the body. However, sprained ankles, sore knees, and stiff necks and backs have also been reported. A number of stories

Exergamers share stories of their misadventures and injuries through Web sites designed specifically for that purpose.

about bumps, bruises, and cuts caused by playing fitness-based video games have appeared in magazines and on Web sites. In fact, a group of serious gamers has started a blog called Wii Have a Problem, where players can post pictures and text about injuries and damages caused by playing games on the Wii system.

Wii Warnings

The Wii video game system comes with a health and safety manual that lists a number of additional injuries that, although

While it rarely occurs, lightning strikes could damage or even destroy an exergame system—and electrocute whoever is holding a controller at the time.

unlikely, could occur. They are:

- Seizures—Nintendo estimates that one out of every four thousand Wii game players might experience a loss of consciousness or involuntary muscle spasms. Sitting far back from the television screen, playing only when well-rested, and making sure there is enough light in the room all help reduce the chance of seizures occurring.
- Eye strain—Eyes are controlled by muscles, which can become strained just like muscles in the arms or legs. Nintendo suggests taking regular breaks and limiting playing time to combat eye strain.
- Electric shock—Wii is an electronic device, so the risk of shock is always present. The same precautions used with other electronics apply here: don't play Wii

games during a lightning storm, don't pull on the cord instead of the plug to disconnect the console, and never use cords or adapters that are damaged.

- Motion sickness—Watching the action on-screen and performing certain maneuvers can make some people dizzy or sick to their stomachs. Stopping the motion, at least for a while, may fix these problems.

How to Avoid Injury

People who like motion-based video games don't have to stop playing in order to avoid injuries, though. There are precautions players can take before, during, and after exergaming that can make participation safe as well as healthy.

Athletes wouldn't take to the field or court without warming up first. Neither should exergamers. Stretching is perhaps the single most important thing a person should do before participating in motion-based video games. Gently moving, warming, and stretching muscles carefully prepares them for energetic play during the game and can help prevent injury. Other precautions include making sure there is enough room to play and removing any breakable items from the playing area. Standing at least 3 feet (1 meter) away from the screen when using the Wii system is recommended as well.

During play, it is wise to follow instructions. For instance, placing the strap of the Wii remote around the wrist, as recommended in the system's users' manual, can significantly reduce injuries and property damage caused by a dropped controller flying through the air. Also, use equipment only as intended.

Securing the Wii controller strap to your wrist, as recommended, lets you play hard while reducing the chance of injury or property damage.

Stepping and standing on the Wii *Fit* balance board is expected, but on-screen text cautions players against jumping on it.

Posture may seem like a strange thing to worry about while playing video games. Yet how a person's body is positioned while it moves can influence the likelihood of an injury occurring. Muscles and tendons that are stretched too far or twisted in unnatural directions are bound to become sore and inflamed. To help players avoid getting hurt, Wii *Fit* and some other exergames have on-screen trainers that demonstrate how moves are to be done. Wii games feature occasional text reminders about posture as well.

Oddly enough, the very thing that makes exergaming so appealing may be the biggest reason for player injuries—motivation. Exercise is good for a person's health, but too much exercise can have a negative effect. Working the body too hard weakens its strength and defenses. People can be so distracted by the fun of playing motion-based video games that they forget to pace themselves. Those who limit their playing time to no more than about an hour at a stretch receive the most health benefits. Resting a while after about half an hour of activity gives the body time to gather more energy and perform better. A Wii *Fit* screen even pops up and suggests that players take a break after a certain amount of playing time.

Myths and Facts

Myth

Nintendo sells the Wii system, especially Wii *Fit*, as a fitness tool.

Fact ➡ The company has never claimed that Wii games are the equivalent of a traditional workout. Nintendo representatives say the system is meant merely to get people active while playing video games.

As long as I'm moving, I'm getting all the exercise I need.

Fact ➡ Movement is exercise, but not all movements are considered equal when it comes to fitness. To get the most benefit from aerobic exercise, the activity should be continuous, or nonstop, for an extended period of time. Doctors and physical fitness experts say at least twenty minutes at a time gets the heart and lungs pumping to levels that do a body good. Also, strength training should be added to aerobic movement for a complete workout.

Playing simulated sports on video game systems is a lot safer than playing actual sports.

Fact ➡ People who play motion-based video games are just as vulnerable to injury as those who play real-life sports and games. Repetitive motion can cause problems no matter where or how it is performed.

HOW BIG A PART SHOULD VIDEO GAMES PLAY IN MY FITNESS ROUTINE?

While motion-based video games are no substitute for actual exercise, they have the ability to reinforce positive, healthy behavior. Through games like those of the Wii system, people are able to sample exercises they may not have attempted before. For instance, someone who is unfamiliar with yoga might enjoy the Wii game poses so much that he or she decides to take a "real" yoga class once a week. Or perhaps someone is interested in tennis but doesn't play because of embarrassment over his or her skill level. Practicing with Wii *Tennis* can increase skills and raise that person's comfort and confidence level enough to get him or her on the court.

The idea that Wii and other active video games could lead to increased physical activity in the real world is not so far-fetched. A 2004 study by Harvard Medical School's

Practicing yoga positions at home with a virtual trainer can be a fun introduction to an actual in-class yoga experience.

Center for Mental Health and Media reported that teenage boys who played sports-related video games were drawn to the traditional versions of those sports as well. Study participants told the Harvard researchers that playing virtual sports on-screen was simply another way of perfecting their skills in an activity they already enjoyed on a regular basis.

Drawing on the strong connection between simulated sports/exercise and the real thing, the question becomes how playing motion-based video games can best be incorporated into a person's fitness activities. The first step would be to figure out what you are trying to accomplish—weight loss, getting stronger or faster—and designing an overall exercise routine that is tailored to your specific needs.

Setting Fitness Goals

When it comes to activity and your health, it might seem like the more the better. Yet overdoing exercise comes with the risk of injury. Therefore, deciding how long and how often you will exercise makes sense. Recommendations from medical and fitness professionals vary.

In its Physical Activity Guidelines for Americans, the U.S. Centers for Disease Control and Prevention (CDC) advises that children and teenagers should be aerobically active for at least one hour every day. The American Presidential Council on Physical Fitness and Sports pushes for one hour of aerobic physical activity as well, but only three days a week. The American College of Sports Medicine offers a kind of compromise, recommending thirty minutes of physical activity most days of the week.

Thirty minutes of concentrated physical activity, done only for the purpose of getting exercise, for three to five days a week is the generally agreed-upon recommendation by medical professionals. Walking to and from school, shopping at the mall, doing chores around the house, or active stuff you do just for fun—like playing motion-based video games—will help fill in the gaps on non-exercise days.

A well-rounded exercise program includes strength training as well as aerobics. The CDC guidelines suggest adding strength

Mowing the lawn is decent calorie-burning exercise. However, it's not nearly as fun as playing fitness-based video games.

training (to build muscle and bone mass) to your exercise routine three times a week. Strength exercises include simple exercises like push-ups, sit-ups, and jumping rope, as well as more involved activities like rock climbing or weight lifting.

The intensity of a workout, meaning the level of effort and energy spent performing the exercise, should be moderate or high. Walking quickly is a moderate-intensity exercise, while high intensity would be the equivalent of running. An easy way to determine intensity level is to take the talk test. Carrying on a conversation during exercise should be a little bit harder than normal, but not extremely difficult or impossible.

Target Heart Rate

A slightly more scientific way to gauge the effectiveness of an exercise routine is by measuring target heart rate. Fitness and health professionals define target heart rate as how fast a person's

Gadgets like this combination watch, calorie-counter, and heart rate monitor make gauging the effectiveness of a workout much less difficult.

heart must pump in order to give him or her the ultimate benefit from exercise, measured as beats per minute. Target heart rate is usually expressed as a percentage of how fast a person's heart could pump, or what's known as the maximum heart rate. Exercising at 100 percent of the maximum heart rate would do more harm than good, so athletes and physical fitness buffs aim for a lower, yet still elevated, rate.

To discover your target heart rate, first subtract your age from the average maximum heart rate, 220 beats per minute. This is your personal maximum heart rate. Your target heart rate is a percentage of your personal heart rate, depending on what you are trying to achieve. Sixty percent of maximum heart rate is the start of the fat burning zone. Eighty percent is the ideal for aerobic exercise. As an example, a ten-year-old's maximum heart rate would be 210 (220 minus 10). At 60 percent of that, or 126 beats per minute, that person would begin to lose weight or at least maintain his or her current weight.

Taking your pulse tells you if you have reached your target heart rate. Stop for a moment in the middle of exercise and hold the fingers of one hand to the inside of your wrist or the side of your neck. Count the number of times you can feel your heart beat for ten seconds, then multiply that by six to determine your number of heartbeats per minute.

Keep in mind that certain medications and medical conditions can affect your heart rate. If you have heart disease, diabetes, or high blood pressure, you should have a doctor determine your target heart rate and even your entire exercise routine. It is recommended that all people beginning a new workout and fitness routine, regardless of their health history, get a medical checkup and consult with their doctor.

Gradual Progress Through Wii

Doctors warn that people should not jump right into exercise at the highest intensity level. Exercise intensity should be increased gradually, a little bit at a time, over many weeks of workouts. A slow, modest start and gradual increases are especially important if you are out of shape or have been almost completely sedentary (inactive).

Starting out slowly on a fitness routine or a new type of exercise is where Wii and other motion-based video games come in handy. Most fitness-based video games provide a low-intensity workout. In other words, a person's heart rate is raised, but not by much and not for long enough periods of time, yet the games still provide suitable health benefits. Low-intensity workouts let beginners and those who are not physically fit build their strength and abilities with a lesser chance of injury. They help them reach the next level of fitness, when higher-intensity traditional workouts can begin.

Some fitness-related video games have built-in safeguards to make sure that eager beginners don't overdo it. For instance, Wii *Fit* is structured so that a set of simple skills in each of the training modes (yoga, balance, strength, aerobics) has to be mastered before any new, harder games are "unlocked" and available to players. Those who are already fit simply have to play the easier, beginner games long enough to unlock the more challenging activities.

Ways to Include Exergaming in Your Fitness Routine

Even people who are skeptical about the benefits of exergaming seem to agree that playing motion-based video games can be a fun and entertaining addition to a traditional fitness routine. Along with stretching, the energetic-yet-low-intensity activity of systems like the Wii make active gaming an excellent form of warm-up, cool-down, or rainy-day exercise. They provide a great way to get in the mood to exercise or reward yourself after working up a sweat.

Motion-based video games are a special form of exercise, so why not make playing them a special event? Get your friends together and play in teams, or make it an individual competition. You could even hold a ceremony and present awards for the best performance in each sport or activity. That's what a

Your doctor can be a useful workout partner simply by offering you good advice and fitness tips, and giving you routine checkups to find out if you're healthy enough to begin an exercise routine.

group of senior citizens in Canada are doing. According to the *National Post* newspaper, residents of retirement communities and long-term care facilities in Toronto are now Wii Olympians. A weeklong tournament featuring Wii *Sports* games, the "Wiilympics," have given these folks a chance to socialize, get active and interested, and improve their physical fitness at the same time.

If you're lucky enough to live in an area that has an XRKade, you can combine going out with your friends with a fun workout. XRKades are clubs filled with the latest exergaming equipment. As of June 2008, there were fifty XRKades in operation across North America, mostly in larger cities. The first international club opened in South Korea that same month.

Any way you choose to enjoy them, fitness-related video games are an exciting exercise option. And if the raging popularity of gaming systems like Nintendo's Wii is any indication, exergaming is a healthy trend that is here to stay.

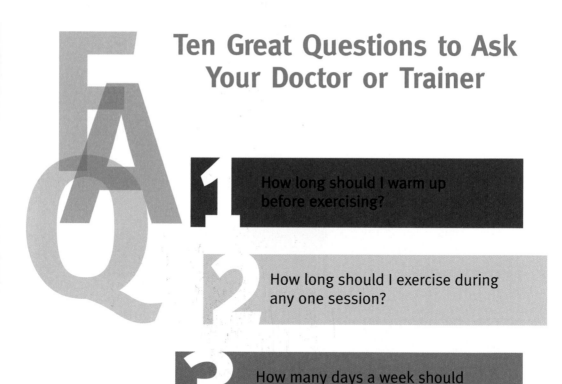

Ten Great Questions to Ask Your Doctor or Trainer

1 How long should I warm up before exercising?

2 How long should I exercise during any one session?

3 How many days a week should I exercise?

4 What type of exercises do you recommend for someone my age, weight, and fitness level?

5 Which exercises or motion-based video games might best help me reach my fitness goals?

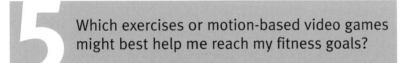

6 What is your opinion on using exergaming to stay fit?

7 Will any of my medications/medical conditions affect my fitness routine?

8 How can I tell if I'm doing a certain exercise correctly?

9 How important are warming up and cooling down before and after workout activity?

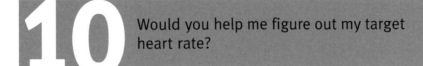

10 Would you help me figure out my target heart rate?

Glossary

aerobic Having to do with activity that works the heart and the lungs.

alveoli Small sacs in the lungs that exchange carbon dioxide for oxygen.

arcade A gallery or space filled with games, both conventional and video.

avatar The on-screen representation of the video game player.

bursitis When bursas—sacs of fluid around the body's joints—swell, causing pain and stiffness.

capillaries Small blood vessels.

cognitive Having to do with thinking and knowledge; relating to the mind and its workings.

exergaming Using technology to make exercise fun; exercise gained through video gaming.

interactive Two-way electronic communication, allowing the user and computer to communicate with each other and respond and react to each other.

isometrics Exercises that build muscle by pushing or pulling against a stationary object.

kinetic Another word for moving; being in motion.

nunchuck A type of controller used to play Wii games.

passive Inactive; unmoving; unresponsive.

peripheral Related but separate; used to describe a piece of add-on video game equipment.

recumbent Reclining; tipped back.

resistance training Working muscles against something that makes their movement harder and therefore more strength-building.

simulated Like the real thing but not quite the same; similar to the real thing, such as a copy or imitation.

strenuous Done with great energy and effort.

tendonitis When tendons become inflamed due to overuse or misuse.

virtual Not actually existing in the "real," physical world; an image or vision that doesn't have tangible, concrete reality.

Active Healthy Kids Canada

2 Bloor Street East, Suite #1804

Toronto, ON M4W 1A8

Canada

(416) 913-0238

Web site: http://www.activehealthykids.ca

Active Healthy Kids Canada is a charitable organization that ensures the importance of quality, accessible, and enjoyable physical activity participation experiences for children and youth through advocacy.

American Council on Exercise (ACE)

4851 Paramount Drive

San Diego, CA 92123

(858) 279-8227

Web site: http://www.acefitness.org

The ACE fights ineffective fitness products, programs, and trends through public education, outreach, trainer certification, and research.

Entertainment Consumers Association (ECA)

64 Danbury Road, Suite 700

Wilton, CT 06897-4406

(203) 761-6180

Web site: http://www.theeca.com

  The ECA is an advocacy organization for consumers of interactive entertainment, focused on promoting consumer rights,
  fighting anti-games legislation, and a host of other public
  policy concerns.

Fitness for Youth
University of Michigan
401 Washtenaw
Ann Arbor, MI 48109-2214
(734) 936-3084
Web site: http://www.fitnessforyouth.umich.edu

  The Fitness for Youth Web site serves as the premier resource
  for information about the health and fitness of America's
  youth. It features innovative and exciting programs to increase
  children's fitness levels; ways to successfully promote physical
  education, activity, and sport in communities; helpful tips
  on running fitness programs; cutting-edge research and
  statistics on children's health; and links to other health-
  oriented Web sites.

U.S. President's Council on Physical Fitness and Sports
Department W
200 Independence Avenue SW
Room 738-H
Washington, DC 20201-0004
(202) 690-9000
Web site: http://www.fitness.gov

The council is an advisory committee of volunteer citizens who advise the president about physical activity, fitness, and sports in America.

YMCA of the USA
101 North Wacker Drive
Chicago, IL 60606
(800) 872-9622
Web site: http://www.ymca.net
  YMCAs are collectively the nation's largest providers of health and well-being programs. They are working to promote healthy living for millions of Americans through YMCA Activate America.

Web Sites

Due to the changing nature of Internet links, Rosen Publishing has developed an online list of Web sites related to the subject of this book. This site is updated regularly. Please use this link to access the list:

http://www.rosenlinks.com/faq/wvif

For Further Reading

Doeden, Matt. *Stay Fit! How You Can Get in Shape.* Minneapolis, MN: Lerner Publishing Group, 2009.

Fairclough, Chris, and Jackie Gaff. *Why Must I Exercise?* London, England: Cherrytree Books, 2005.

Kennedy, Rose R., ed. *The Family Fitness Fun Book: Healthy Living for the Whole Family.* Long Island City, NY: Hatherleigh Press, 2005.

Orland, Kyle. *Wii for Dummies.* Indianapolis, IN: Wiley Publishing, Inc., 2008.

Prima Games. *Wii Fit Training Companion: Prima Official Game Guide.* New York, NY: Random House, 2008.

Shannon, Joyce Brennfleck. *Sports Injuries Information for Teens: Health Tips About Sports Injuries and Injury Prevention.* Detroit, MI: Omnigraphics, Inc., 2003.

Sothern, Melinda S., et al. *Trim Kids: The Proven 12-Week Plan That Has Helped Thousands of Children Achieve a Healthier Weight.* New York, NY: Collins Living, 2003.

Trueit, Trudi Strain. *Video Gaming.* North Mankato, MN: Cherry Lake Publishing, 2008.

Yoshizumi, Carol. *Real Fitness: 101 Games and Activities to Get Girls Going!* (American Girl Library). Middleton, WI: American Girl Publishing, 2006.

Index

A

aerobic exercise, 11, 12, 14,
    18–20, 21, 23, 29, 45, 48
American Council on Exercise
    (ACE), 29
anaerobic exercise, 22
arcade games, 6, 12
avatars, 10, 14

B

balance boards, 9
body mass index (BMI), 31
Brain Age, 25
bursitis, 38

C

calisthenics, 23
calorie calculators, 12
carpal tunnel syndrome, 38
Cateye Fitness, 12
Centers for Disease Control
    and Prevention (CDC), 48
CogniFit, 25
cool-down exercises, 52, 55

D

Dance Dance Revolution, 6,
    11–12
diabetes, 51
digital cameras, 15
doctor/trainer, ten great
    questions to ask your, 54–55

E

electric shock, 41–42
exergaming, 7, 9, 12, 14, 27,
    28, 30–32, 36, 42, 44, 55
Exer-Station, 14
eye strain, 41
EyeToy, 15

F

Fisher-Price, 13

G

GameBike, 12
GameRunner, 13
GameVision, 21

H

heart disease, 51
heart rate, target, 55, 49–51
high blood pressure, 51

I

isometrics, 14

M

MindFit, 25
motion sickness, 42
My Weight Loss Coach, 21

N

Nintendo, 5, 9, 21, 25, 41, 44, 54
nunchucks, 9, 10
nutritionists, 7, 31

P

PC games, 13
physical therapists, 7, 32–33
PlayStation, 11

R

repetitive strain injuries (RSIs), 35

S

seizures, 41
Smart Cycle, 13
stationary bikes, 6, 12, 20
strength training, 18, 21–23, 49

T

ten great questions to ask your doctor/trainer, 54
tendonitis, 37–38
tennis elbow, 37
treadmills, 6, 7, 13, 20

U

Ubisoft, 21
U.S. Presidential Council on Physical Fitness, 23

V

video fitness
    and age, 5, 11, 13, 26, 32, 54
    blogging about, 30–32, 40
    definition of, 4–5
    drawbacks of, 7, 34–44
    myths/facts about, 44–45
    and rehabilitation, 5, 32–33
    vs. traditional exercise, 7, 26–33, 45, 46–49
    and weight loss, 20–21, 26, 30–32, 48
    and Wii, 5–6, 9–11, 14, 19, 21, 23, 26, 28, 29, 30, 32, 35, 37, 40–44, 46, 52, 54
video games
    active vs. passive, 16, 17–18, 19, 26–28
    and injuries, 7, 34–44
    and mental fitness, 24–25

W

warm-up exercises, 52, 55
webcams, 15
WebMD, 31
Wii *Fit*, 5, 10, 14, 23, 24, 26, 32, 43, 44, 52
Wii Have a Problem, 40
Wii *Sports*, 10, 14, 19, 26, 28, 29, 30, 32, 35, 53

X

Xbox, 11

About the Author

Jeanne Nagle is a journalist and writer from Rochester, New York. Among other titles she's written for Rosen is *What Happens to Your Body When You Swim*. Her favorite part of researching this book has been trying out several of the games and equipment mentioned herein with her family and friends.

Photo Credits

Cover, p. 8 © www.istockphoto.com; p. 5 © James Keyser/Time & Life Pictures/Getty Images; p. 6 © AP Photos; pp. 10, 33 © Ralph Orlowski/Getty Images; pp. 13, 15, 19 © Newscom; p. 17 © Michael Newman/Photo Edit; p. 20 © Scott Barbour/Getty Images; p. 22 © Bob Riha Jr./WireImage/Getty Images; p. 25 © Fred Prouser/Reuters/Landov; p. 29 © www.istockphoto.com/ Stephan Hoerold; p. 31 © Ryan Collard/New York Times/Redux Pictures; p. 35 © Gary Connor/Phototake; p. 37 © Custom Medical Stock Photo; p. 39 © www.istockphoto.com/Arman Zhenikeyev; p. 41 © www.istockphoto.com/Jeff Chevrier; p. 43 © Syracuse Newspapers/S. Cannerelli/The Image Works; p. 47 © www.istockphoto.com/Eliza Snow; p. 49 © www. istockphoto.com/Randolph Pamphrey; p. 50 Yoshikazu Tsuno/ Getty Images; p. 53 © www.istockphoto.com.

Designer: Nicole Russo; Photo Researcher: Marty Levick